# Laughing Your Way Through the A+ Certification

*Jokes, Puns and Groaners and more for the IT Aspirant*

## By Alan Gorithm

*"Remember, in the world of IT, if you don't laugh at the absurdity of rebooting a machine for the third time, you'll just end up crying at the tragedy of it all. So keep your humor close and your knowledge closer—both are equally essential for survival in the silicon jungle!"*

*—Anita Upgrade*

# Copyright © 2023

# Disclaimer

"This book, titled 'Laughing Your Way Through the A+ Certification—Jokes, Puns and Groaners for the IT Aspirant,' is an independent publication and has not been authorized, sponsored, or otherwise approved by CompTIA. The content within this book is provided for comedic and entertainment purposes only and does not constitute an official study guide for the CompTIA A+ certification exams.

All trademarks, service marks, trade names, trade dress, product names, and logos appearing in this book are the property of their respective owners and are used for identification purposes only. Use of these terms, and the content of this book, does not imply any affiliation with or endorsement by their respective trademark holders.

The information in this book is provided 'as is' without any express or implied warranty. The views expressed by the author, Al Gorithm, are solely their own and do not reflect the views of CompTIA or any other certification body. While humor is the heart of the text, the author makes no representations or warranties with respect to the accuracy or completeness of the contents and specifically disclaims any implied warranties of merchantability or fitness for a particular purpose.

No part of this book should be taken as legal or professional advice for passing the CompTIA A+ certification exams. Readers should use this book as a supplement to official study materials and are encouraged to consult CompTIA's official resources for exam preparation.

The author and publisher shall not be liable for any loss of profit or any other commercial damages, including but not limited to special, incidental, consequential, or other damages."

# Table of Contents

# Dedication

To the tireless seekers of digital truth,
The midnight oil burners, the relentless youth.
To the mentors with wisdom, endlessly shared,
And the students with eyes, brightly flared.

To the keyboard warriors, in caffeine we trust,
To the servers, the routers, the towers of dust.
To the bytes, to the bits, to the endless loops,
To the tangled cables, and the data groups.

To the ones who've ever lost a file,
And found it again, after a while.
To the unsung heroes fixing a motherboard's plight,
With nothing but a dim desk lamp's light.

And to you, the reader, with this book in your hand,
May your laughter be loud and your A+ grand.
For every groan at a pun that's made,
Remember, it's just another step in the upgrade.

By Al Gorithm,
In honor of every IT journey begun,
And in memory of the paper manuals now gone.
May your path be clear and your code never lag,
And may your spirits be as high as your bandwidth is broad.

# Foreword: Why Humor Makes for Memorable IT

Welcome, tech enthusiasts, future IT experts, and seekers of laughter! You hold in your hands (or on your screens) a unique tool—an A+ Certification study guide that's wired a bit differently. Here, we subscribe to the notion that laughter isn't just the best medicine; it's also the best teacher.

**The Power of Laughter in Learning**

Why humor? Because studies have shown that when we laugh, we relax, and when we're relaxed, we're more open to learning. Laughter reduces stress and increases retention. It breaks down walls, making those intimidating technical concepts seem more approachable. Plus, who doesn't want to chuckle while deciphering the cryptic language of tech?

Humor has a way of making things stick. Remember the last time you laughed at a joke? You probably still recall the punchline. Now imagine if every key concept of the A+ Certification came with a guffaw, a giggle, or at least a grin. That's our mission: to make the critical points of IT support memorable through humor.

**How This Book is Structured**

This isn't your typical, dry textbook that drones on in a monotone of technical jargon. No, it's a vibrant collection of jokes, stories, and lighthearted banter, all meticulously designed to align with the A+ exam objectives.

Each chapter opens with a joke or a funny anecdote that introduces the topic. As you delve deeper, you'll find key learning points interwoven with humor. Don't worry; the laughs aren't just for show—they're carefully crafted to highlight the essentials you need to know.

At the end of each chapter, we'll circle back to ensure the key points have not only been presented but presented in a way that will make them stick. Like the surprise twist in a good joke, we'll give you that "aha" moment that makes the learning memorable.

So prepare to laugh your way through learning. Let's turn those frowns upside down and those complex IT concepts inside out. By the time you're done, you'll not only be ready to ace the A+ Certification but also be the life of the IT department party. And remember, in the world of technology, where the only constant is change, a sense of humor is the best toolkit you can carry.

Now, let's boot up and crack up as we embark on this journey of jokes and jargon!

# Chapter 1: The Boot-Up Laugh Sequence

Welcome to the first chapter of your journey to becoming A+ Certified, peppered with a generous sprinkle of tech humor to start your engines—or should we say, to start your systems!

**Introduction to A+ Certification**

Before we dive into the comedic circuitry of IT, let's understand what the A+ Certification is all about. It's like the Hogwarts School of Witchcraft and Wizardry for IT professionals—except instead of spells and potions, you get hard drives and protocols. And there's no Sorting Hat here, just a set of exams that sort the tech wizards from the muggles.

Think of A+ Certification as your passport into the world of IT. It's the first step on a journey filled with troubleshooting, networking, security, and so much more. It's the foundation upon which you can build a rock-solid IT career. And like any good foundation, it's as sturdy as the knowledge it's built upon—knowledge that we're about to make stick with the help of a few laughs.

**The Funniest PC Startup and Booting Blunders**

Have you heard about the computer that was so slow to boot up, it displayed a "To be continued..." message on the screen? Or what about the PC that was so old, it had a separate key just for Ctrl-Alt-Delete? Booting blunders are the bread and butter of IT comedy. From the 'blue screen of death' that's more like the 'blue screen of "time for a coffee break"' to the startup sounds that become the soundtrack of a tech's nightmares, there's no shortage of hilarity when a computer just won't start right.

Picture this: An IT tech walks into a bar and the bartender asks, "Why the long POST?" The tech replies, "Because the BIOS is telling bad boot jokes again!"

**Key Concepts: BIOS/UEFI, POST, and Boot Sequence**

Now, let's get serious—just kidding, let's get educational. BIOS and UEFI are the backstage managers of your computer's boot-up performance. BIOS, the Basic Input/Output System, is like the computer's subconscious, handling the basics before the conscious mind of the OS kicks in. UEFI, or Unified Extensible Firmware Interface, is its modern cousin, with more features, faster boot times, and better security. It's the BIOS after it went to the gym and got a makeover.

Then there's the POST, which stands for Power-On Self-Test, not "post" as in, "I'll post a selfie of my computer freezing again." It's the system's way of making sure everything is in check before the main event. If POST were a person, it'd be that friend who double-checks if you've got your keys, wallet, and phone before leaving the house.

The boot sequence, meanwhile, is the process your computer follows to get from "off" to "ready to rock and roll." It's the startup playlist, the sequence of steps your system takes to get the party started. And like any good playlist, it can be customized in the settings, though be warned—tinkering with it is like remixing a classic hit. It might boot faster, or it might just crash and burn.

By the end of this chapter, not only will you understand these concepts, but you'll also have a few jokes to boot (pun intended). So let's raise the curtain and power up the laughter because we're about to boot up some serious learning!

# Chapter 2: Hardware Hilarity

Strap in and prepare for a tour of your computer's inner sanctum, where the hardware hangs out. It's like a house party in your PC, and every component has its own personality and punchline.

## Motherboards: The Main Event

Why did the motherboard blush? Because it saw the CPU and RAM clocking together! The motherboard is like the host of the hardware party—it connects all the components. It's also the biggest gossip in the PC; it knows everything that's going on, from the CPU's workload to the latest drama in the expansion slots.

Did you hear about the claustrophobic motherboard? It didn't have enough space for its RAM friends, so it expanded its DIMM slots. Now, that's what we call memory improvement!

## CPUs: The Brains and the Brawn

How many CPUs does it take to change a light bulb? Just one, but it'll take a million cycles to do it! The CPU, or Central Processing Unit, is the brain of the computer. If it were a kitchen appliance, it would be the blender—mixing up instructions to make the smoothie of operations that keep your system running.

Remember, if your CPU could talk, it would say, "Keep cool, folks," because a hot-headed CPU is a no-go. It's all about staying chill under pressure—or should we say, under a heatsink.

## RAM: Forget Me Not

How do you know when your RAM is in a good mood? When it's feeling randomly accessible! RAM, or Random Access Memory, is the forgetful genius of your computer. It's brilliant while it's on, remembering everything the CPU tells it, but the moment the power goes off, it's all, "What was I doing again?"

Why don't you ever play hide and seek with your RAM? Because the moment you turn around, it forgets it's playing!

**Hard Drives: Memory Lane**

Why was the hard drive always invited to parties? Because it knows how to save the good times! Hard drives are the keepers of your digital treasures—the photos, the documents, the unending abyss of memes. They're like that friend who has a photo from every event ever but takes a minute to find it.

You know your hard drive is getting old when it starts making that "whrrr-click" sound. That's the tech equivalent of "back in my day…"

**Power Supplies: The Unsung Heroes**

Power supplies don't get many jokes; they're the unsung heroes of the PC world. But remember, without a power supply, your PC is just a very expensive paperweight.

Did you hear about the power supply that went to therapy? It had too many volts of emotions and needed to convert them into a stable output!

By the end of this chapter, not only will you laugh at the quirks of each piece of hardware, but you'll also understand their critical roles in your computer's ecosystem. And the next time your computer has a hiccup, you'll know exactly which partygoer to have a chat with. So let's giggle our way through gigabytes and make some memorable motherboard mirth!

# Chapter 3: Hilarious Hardware Troubleshooting

Prepare to dive into the belly laughs of the beast where the screws and capacitors meet the punchlines. Troubleshooting hardware is like being a detective in a comedy club—every clue has a joke attached.

## Comedic Troubleshooting Scenarios

Have you heard about the technician who brought a rubber chicken to a troubleshooting job? He heard it was good to have a "fowl-safe" plan. Troubleshooting is about expecting the unexpected—like finding a motherboard that's afraid of heights or a hard drive that's decided to go on a read-only diet.

Why did the PC get cold? Because Windows was left open! And why did the computer take a nap? Because it had too many sleepless "bytes." When you're troubleshooting, it's not just about asking what's wrong; it's about asking what pun is right.

## Key Concepts: Diagnostic Procedures

Why did the tech bring a duck to work? For its expert web-footed diagnostics! Just like a duck takes to water, a good tech takes to diagnostic procedures. Remember, when you're running diagnostics, you're not just looking for problems—you're looking for a good time!

A computer once went to the doctor and said, "Doc, I think I've come down with a virus!" The doctor replied, "Have you tried running in safe mode?" Yes, sometimes the solution is that simple, and other times, you're deciphering beep codes that sound like Morse code from a sarcastic telegraph.

## Error Codes: The Language of Sighs

Error codes are like the computer's way of saying, "I've got a joke for you, but you're going to have to work for it." They're the cryptic punchlines to jokes we didn't know were being told. Have you met the infamous "404"? That's the computer's way of playing hide and seek.

And who can forget the classic "blue screen of death"? It's like the computer's dramatic way of saying, "I can't even!" But don't worry, with this guide, you'll turn those tragic moments into comedic gold.

**Common Issues: The Usual Suspects**

Let's talk about the usual suspects of hardware hiccups. Like the printer that won't print—it's either out of ink, on strike, or just has a paper jam session. Or the keyboard that starts typing cryptic messages—it's not haunted, it's just got sticky keys from that time you ate a donut while emailing.

Remember the tech who fixed a "no display" issue by simply turning on the monitor? Sometimes the problems are as plain as the nose on your face—unless you've got a face without a nose, which is a whole different troubleshooting chapter.

By the time you're done with this chapter, you'll not only be the Sherlock Holmes of hardware issues, but you'll also be the life of the IT party, regaling your colleagues with tales of troubleshooting tribulations and triumphs. So, let's grab our diagnostic tools and our joke books and get to solving!

# Chapter 4: Operating System Oddities

Welcome to the whimsical world of operating systems, where every installation is an adventure and every update is a punchline waiting to happen. Let's navigate the quirks and features of OS management with a smirk.

## The Lighter Side of OS Installation, Configuration, and Upgrading

Installing an operating system is like telling a joke: timing is everything. Have you ever tried installing Windows on a Friday the 13th? It's like the OS senses your fear and decides to throw in a plot twist—like a sudden reboot when you're just about to finish.

And then there's configuring your new OS. It's like arranging a first date; you want to make a good impression, but you also don't want to show all the annoying pop-ups too soon. Or the endless updates: "Your system will reboot several times," it says, like a tech version of Groundhog Day.

### Windows Wackiness

Windows is the extrovert of operating systems—always updating, always changing, and always asking if you'd like to restart now or wait another hour. It's the friend who says, "I'll just pop by for a minute," and is still there hours later, updating.

Why don't Windows PCs work well at the North Pole? Because every time Santa logs on, Windows freezes! And have you heard about the new restaurant called 'Windows'? It's got great menus, but you can't exit without going through several prompts first.

### Mac OS Quirks

Mac OS is the sleek, fashionable one in the OS group. It's like that friend who shows up impeccably dressed and sometimes, just sometimes, forgets that you don't own a MacBook to appreciate all its accessories.

What do you call a Mac that's acting up? An iMoody. And why did the Mac user cross the road? To get to the Apple Store for another dongle, obviously.

**Linux Larks**

Ah, Linux, the DIY enthusiast of operating systems. It's the one you go to when you want to prove you can build your own furniture—I mean, set up your own server.

How do you know someone uses Linux? Don't worry; they'll tell you. And why do Linux users never get lost? Because they always find their way around the terminal!

**File Systems Funnies**

File systems are like the secret diaries of your OS. NTFS, FAT32, exFAT—they're all just different ways of keeping your digital life in order. FAT32 is the old-school journal, NTFS is the encrypted diary, and exFAT is the blog for all devices.

Why don't file systems get along at parties? Because they have different formats for addressing issues. And what do you call a file system that can't decide on its format? Disk-organized.

**Command Line Chuckles**

The command line: a place where you can feel like a wizard or a muggle, depending on the day. It's the text-based underbelly where you can make magic happen with just a few keystrokes—assuming you've remembered the incantations correctly.

Why do command line users make terrible comedians? Because they always think in terms of "execute"! And what did one command line say to the other? "You complete me."

By the end of this chapter, you won't just be adept at navigating the peculiarities of operating systems—you'll also be armed with a bevy of tech jests to lighten the mood whenever a loading screen dares to test your patience. Ready to upgrade your humor OS? Let's boot up the banter!

# Chapter 5: Networking Nonsense

Step into the world of networking, where every connection is an opportunity for comedy, and the only thing more tangled than the cables are the punchlines. Ready to configure your chuckles? Let's connect!

**Amusing Anecdotes about Network Configuration and Troubleshooting**

Network configuration is like a dance: sometimes it's a smooth waltz, other times it's the Macarena with two left feet. Take the time I told a router to find the shortest path, and it rerouted through the kitchen—because that's where the cookies are!

And then there's Wi-Fi, the magical invisible force that binds all our devices. It's like fairy dust, except when it stops working, then it's just dust. Why did the computer go to therapy? Because it had too many unresolved connections.

Troubleshooting networks is like being in a relationship: it's all about communication, and sometimes you have to reset to make things work again. Remember the network tech who used a stethoscope? He said he was listening for "packet heartbeats."

**Key Concepts: TCP/IP**

TCP/IP is the postal service of the internet, but instead of letters, we're sending packets. And just like the mail, sometimes packets get lost, and you have to send them again. TCP is that reliable mailman who always gets a signature, while UDP is his cousin who just leaves packages on the porch and hopes for the best.

How does TCP flirt? It says, "Are you sure you got all of this?" UDP just says, "I don't care if you got it, I'm moving on!"

**Wi-Fi Standards**

Wi-Fi standards are like fashion trends: as soon as you get the latest, a new one comes out. First, we had 802.11b, then 802.11g, and now we're up to 802.11ax. It's like the alphabet soup of connectivity—delicious, but confusing.

Why did the Wi-Fi and the computer break up? Because the computer had too many wires attached!

## SOHO Networks

SOHO networks are like the mom-and-pop shops of networking. They're small, they're personal, and they know all the devices by name. Why don't SOHO networks make good comedians? Because they can't handle too many streams!

## Routing

Routers are the traffic cops of the network world, directing packets where to go. But sometimes they get a little power-hungry. How do routers say goodbye? "It's been nice packet-ing with you!"

Why was the router stressed out? Because it had too many conflicting routes, like a GPS with a split personality!

By the end of this chapter, you won't just be able to navigate the networking labyrinth—you'll be the Minotaur, ruling over it with an iron fist and a joke book. So, let's dive into the network narrative and emerge as the lords of the LANs, jesters of the routers, and sultans of the switches!

# Chapter 6: Security Snickers

Get ready to lock down the laughs in a chapter where cybersecurity gets a comic twist. Remember, the only thing we're infecting here are your funny bones!

**Security Gone Silly: Understanding Cybersecurity with a Smile**

Cybersecurity is serious business, but that doesn't mean we can't have a giggle as we guard the gates. Think of your firewall like a nightclub bouncer—it's tough, it's selective, and it's not letting anyone shady through without the right credentials.

And passwords? They're like the secret handshakes of the digital world. The problem is, some folks treat them like a "Hello, my name is" sticker. "Password123," really? That's the handshake equivalent of a limp fish.

**Key Concepts: Malware Types**

Malware types are like the villains in a spy movie. You've got the viruses, the sneaky little bugs that sneak in with a sniffle and leave with your files. Then there are the trojans, masquerading as harmless software while plotting to take over your digital kingdom.

Why did the malware go to school? To improve its "phishing" skills! And ransomware? That's the digital kidnapper, holding your files at ransom until you cough up the crypto. It's no wonder they say, "Don't click on shady links!" It's the virtual equivalent of taking candy from strangers.

**Authentication Methods**

Authentication is all about proving you are who you say you are. There's something poetic about a system asking, "Who goes there?" like a knight at a castle gate. And biometrics? That's just fancy talk for your computer getting all personal, like a tech-savvy grandma saying, "I'd recognize that fingerprint anywhere!"

Why do biometric systems make terrible stand-up comedians? Because they can't handle multiple users!

**Encryption**

Encryption is the secret code of the internet. It's like writing in invisible ink—unless you have the UV light of decryption, it's all just gibberish. It's what keeps eavesdroppers out of your digital conversations. Without encryption, sending sensitive data is like sending a postcard—everyone can read about Aunt Marge's bunion surgery.

Why did the hacker break up with encryption? It said it needed space, but really, it couldn't find the key!

By the time you're done with this chapter, you'll be cracking codes and jokes with equal skill. You'll be the one at the water cooler saying, "I'll tell you a UDP joke, but you might not get it." So let's secure our knowledge and our networks, and remember: the only thing we're phishing for here is laughter!

# Chapter 7: Software Shenanigans

Step right up to the whimsical world of software, where the only bugs are in the code and the only crashes happen on virtual racetracks. Let's debug some humor with a side of savvy software management!

## Laughing Through Software Management and Troubleshooting

Picture this: you're trying to uninstall a program that's as clingy as an overfed cat. It's supposed to be gone, but somehow it's still there, popping up at startup asking, "Did you miss me?" That's software management in a nutshell—sometimes you're the cat owner, sometimes you're the scratched-up furniture.

Troubleshooting software is like being in a sitcom where the plot is a never-ending loop of "Have you tried turning it off and on again?" It's the classic line, the 'dad joke' of the IT world, and guess what? Most of the time, it works like a charm, much to the chagrin of sophisticated techies everywhere.

## Key Concepts: Operating Systems

Operating systems are like the personalities of computers. You've got Windows, the multitasking busybody; macOS, the sleek artiste; Linux, the free-spirited tinkerer; and Chrome OS, the cloud-dwelling minimalist. They're the Spice Girls of software, each with its own flair and fanbase.

Why did the operating system apply for a job? It wanted to make sure it had "Windows" of opportunity. And what does an operating system snack on? "Cookies" and "chips."

## Application Software

Application software is the personal trainer for your computer, specialized in everything from word processing biceps to spreadsheet abs. They're the tools that turn your PC from a glorified typewriter into a powerhouse of productivity.

Why did the spreadsheet file go to therapy? Because it had too many "cell" issues. And let's not forget about the antivirus software—it's the digital equivalent of a bodyguard, except instead of sunglasses and a suit, it's rocking code and firewalls.

**Mobile OS**

Mobile operating systems are the pocket-sized life coaches. They keep your digital life organized on the go, whether it's Android juggling your apps like a circus performer or iOS keeping your data as tight as a snare drum.

Ever wonder why mobile games are so addictive? They're engineered by software wizards who know that the only thing faster than a quick level is our willingness to procrastinate.

In the realm of software shenanigans, whether you're sailing through seamless updates or navigating the treacherous waters of "Error 404," remember: the best bug is the one you can laugh about... after you've fixed it, of course. So let's get ready to tickle our tech-savvy sensibilities and wrangle some software into submission—with a smile!

# Chapter 8: Mobile Madness

Dive into the pocket-sized pandemonium where mobile devices reign supreme and the mishaps are as common as missed group text notifications. Welcome to the hilarious hustle and bustle of Mobile Madness!

**Mobile Device Mishaps and Humor**

Why did the smartphone go to school? Because it lost its "Intel"! Mobile devices are like the Swiss Army knives of the digital age: they can do anything, except when they mysteriously run out of space—then they can't even update an app without a full-blown digital detox.

Ever noticed how a dropped phone seems to fall in slow motion? It's as if even gravity has a twisted sense of humor. And those moments when you're frantically tapping the screen during a freeze? That's the modern-day equivalent of a rain dance, hoping for the benevolent tech gods to restore order.

**Key Concepts: iOS**

iOS is like the well-dressed guest at the party who doesn't need a name tag. It's smooth, it's sophisticated, and it keeps your life in a neatly organized album—whether you asked for it or not. It's also got a VIP section in its App Store, and sometimes, it seems like apps need to know a secret handshake to get in.

Android Antics

Android, on the other hand, is the life of the party, welcoming all sorts of apps with open arms. It's customizable like a Build-A-Bear, with widgets and settings galore. Android users love freedom—the freedom to customize, to choose, and to use their phones as remote controls, digital wallets, or mini boomboxes.

**Synchronization Symphony**

Synchronization is the unsung symphony that keeps your digital life in harmony. It's like a maestro conducting an orchestra of devices, ensuring that your music, photos, and contacts are in sync. But when it goes wrong, it's like a flash mob where everyone forgot the moves.

Why don't devices ever get out of sync at a good time? Because perfect harmony is for concerts, not for the chaos of our daily tech lives.

**Mobile Security Skits**

Mobile security is like an overprotective parent—it means well, but sometimes it can be a little too much. Ever had your phone ask for a fingerprint, a password, and a DNA sample just to check the weather? That's mobile security, always trying to keep your digital life safe from the playground bullies of malware and hackers.

Remember, in the world of mobile devices, your phone knows you better than your best friend, and sometimes, that's the scariest joke of all.

So, as you swipe through your apps and tap away messages on your digital sidekick, remember to enjoy the quirks and laugh at the snafus. After all, it's not a bug; it's a feature—of the comedy that is Mobile Madness!

# Chapter 9: Operational Hilarity

Welcome to the world of operational IT, where the punchlines are as important as the protocols, and every ticket closed is a story worth telling—at least with a little comedic embellishment.

**Professional IT Practices with a Punchline**

Professional IT practices are no joke—but the situations we encounter? Now those are comedy gold. For instance, there's the age-old tale of the user who thought "net working" involved a fishing trip. Or the client who insisted their cup holder was broken, only to learn it was actually a CD tray.

And let's not forget the "Have you tried turning it off and on again?" mantra. It's the IT version of "take two aspirin and call me in the morning," and nine times out of ten, it works like a charm—much to the chagrin of clients who expect a more "advanced" solution.

**Key Concepts: Customer Service**

Customer service in IT is like being a therapist, but for computers— and sometimes their users. It's all about listening, empathizing, and occasionally, talking people through plugging in their "unresponsive" monitors. The real trick is maintaining a straight face when you solve a problem by plugging in the "unplugged" device.

Did you hear about the IT technician who won an award for customer service? He had all the "connections."

**Documentation: The IT Diary**

Documentation is the diary of the IT world, except instead of secrets, it's filled with configurations, settings, and those "I fixed it but I have no idea how" moments. Good documentation is like a treasure map—it leads you right to the "X" that marks the spot, where "X" is the fix that saves the day.

Why do IT techs keep detailed logs? So they can remember all the times they saved the digital world before lunchtime.

**Safety Procedures: The Comedy of Caution**

Safety procedures in IT are crucial, and sometimes, they're as straightforward as using a surge protector to save your computer from a lightning storm. Other times, they're as complex as explaining to a user why "password" is not a safe password.

Safety first, they say, because nothing's funnier than a tech who forgot to ground themselves before handling components. Static electricity: it's not just a shock, it's a punchline.

In the land of operational IT, every day is a new scene in the sitcom of tech life. So, remember to follow the protocols, keep your documentation close, and always, always keep your sense of humor at the ready. After all, laughter might not be included in the official IT toolkit, but it's just as essential.

# Chapter 10: The Joy of Tech Support

Step into the call center arena, where the headsets are on and the mute button is off. It's time to navigate the delightful chaos of tech support, where every call is a curtain opening on a potential comedy sketch.

## Tech Support Transcripts That Tickle the Funny Bone

Imagine a tech support call where the user insists their wireless router isn't working, and after an hour of troubleshooting, you discover they thought "wireless" meant it didn't need to be plugged into a power source. Or the classic case of the user who complained about a "dead" laptop that simply had its brightness turned all the way down.

Why was the computer cold in the house? Because Windows was left open! And why did the smartphone go to the party solo? It lost its "pairing."

## Key Concepts: Troubleshooting Methodology

Troubleshooting is like being a detective with a magnifying glass, except instead of fingerprints, you're looking for misplaced commas in code or the elusive "user error." It's a process—a beautiful, sometimes maddening, always rewarding process.

Why did the tech support agent cross the road? To troubleshoot the traffic light's network connection on the other side, of course!

## Remote Support: The Virtual Comedy Club

Remote support is the realm where tech magicians perform their spells over the airwaves. It's a place where "Can you please go to the start menu" turns into a 20-minute exercise in explaining what the "start menu" is, and that indeed, it has nothing to do with starting the user's car.

Have you heard about the remote tech who developed a cure for computer viruses? He called it "Chicken Soup for the Motherboard."

In tech support, the laughs are plenty, the satisfaction of a job well done is real, and the stories... well, they're as endless as the queue of incoming calls. So let's embrace the joy, the jokes, and the gentle art of asking, "Have you tried restarting your device?"

# Chapter 11: Peripheral Puns

Welcome to the side-show of the main computing act, the world of peripherals, where the supporting characters are just as important (and hilarious) as the leads. Let's plug into the comedy with devices that bring new meaning to the term 'plug and play'.

**Side-Splitting Scenarios Involving Printers, Monitors, and More**

Have you ever witnessed a printer rebellion? It begins with one paper jam and ends with a toner cartridge explosion that looks like a black-and-white Jackson Pollock. Printers, the cats of peripherals—they do as they please, and when they finally work, they act like they're doing you a favor.

Then there are the monitors, the windows to our computer's soul. Some are like clear, blue skies; others, more like a foggy day in London town, especially after you've accidentally changed the resolution to 800x600.

And who can forget the scanners? They've seen more awkward office moments than the water cooler. Ever tried scanning your face for a laugh? Just remember, the result is always more 'haunted house' than 'Vanity Fair'.

**Key Concepts: Types of Peripherals**

In the vast ecosystem of peripherals, you have the input legends: keyboards and mice, the unsung heroes typing out the symphonies of spreadsheets and navigating the seas of the internet. They're the reliable sidekicks, until the coffee spill disaster turns your keyboard into a sticky-note mosaic.

Speakers and headphones are the bards of the peripheral world, each singing the ballads of your playlists. But beware the volume settings—they've been known to orchestrate jump scares better than any horror movie.

Webcams, the watchful eyes, allow us to connect face-to-pixelated-face with friends, family, and colleagues. They've made our chins famous and our ceilings the most viewed scenes in our homes.

## Installation and Maintenance

Installing a new peripheral is like adopting a pet. You need to introduce it slowly to its new environment, ensure the right drivers are in place, and sometimes, give it a name. "This is Jerry, my third mouse this year; the wheel keeps getting stuck."

Maintenance is the ongoing saga of updates, cleaning, and the occasional tender pep talk to coax a little more life out of an aging device. It's the tech equivalent of watering plants, except sometimes you need compressed air and firmware updates rather than water and sunlight.

By now, you've probably realized that peripherals are more than just accessories; they're the lifeblood of our interaction with technology. They can make us laugh with their quirks and frustrate us with their caprices, but in the end, we'd be lost in a sea of unprinted documents, silent movies, and untyped words without them. So here's to the peripherals, the jesters in the court of computing—may they continue to amuse and serve us, in all their whimsical glory.

# Chapter 12: The IT Crowd – Comedic Client Interactions

Enter the stage of the IT support world, where the interactions are as unpredictable as a roll of the dice and every support ticket tells a story worthy of a sitcom episode. Here we spotlight the hilarity that ensues when the IT crowd meets the end-user ensemble.

**True Tales from the IT Frontlines, with a Humorous Twist**

There's the legendary tale of the executive who used his CD tray as a cup holder, leading to a java-scripted disaster. Or the intrepid user who called complaining about her "wireless cable not reaching far enough"—a paradox that left even the seasoned tech scratching his head.

Then there was the support call that echoed with the sound of typing... only to discover the client was using the keyboard as a footrest. It's true, in the land of IT, reality often trumps fiction.

But let's not forget the triumphs, like the time a tech explained the cloud so well, the client looked out the window expecting to see their data float by. Or the day someone thanked IT for making their computer "go fast again" after cleaning up the desktop icons.

**Key Concepts: Professionalism**

Professionalism in IT is the art of keeping a straight face when a client says they've tried turning it "off and on" when they actually just flicked the monitor's power button. It's about delivering service with a smile, even when the hundredth "urgent" email of the day asks why the computer won't turn on, with the power strip clearly showing no signs of life.

It's mastering the poker voice when on the phone: "Yes, ma'am, I understand your spreadsheet is vital, but your cat walking on the keyboard isn't what we mean by 'debugging' the system."

**Communication**

Communication is key, they say, and never is it truer than in IT. It's the bridge between "Did you try restarting?" and "Let me explain why we don't use a hammer to fix the printer." Clear communication is often the difference between a resolved ticket and a client using their laptop as a pricey paperweight.

Consider the tech who taught metaphors to better explain malware: "Think of it like the flu for your computer, and yes, it can be contagious."

**Client Education**

Client education is the unsung hero of IT. It's one part teaching, two parts patience, and sometimes, a pinch of comedy. Like when you explain that the "any" key isn't a magical button, or that phishing doesn't involve a rod and reel.

But the true victory is when clients start using terms correctly. That's when you know they've graduated from the school of IT support, ready to face the world wide web, armed with more than just a sticky note covering their webcam.

In the end, the IT crowd knows that each call, each question, is more than just a task—it's an episode in the grand tech series, where the laughs are plenty and the learning never stops. So, let's toast to the helpdesks and the troubleshooters, the digital wizards, and the patient explainers—they're not just IT professionals; they're the narrators of our digital stories.

# Chapter 13: Laughable Laws of Computing

In the motherboard of life, computing laws are the quirks programmed into the system. Let's explore the Murphy's Law of IT, where if something can go wrong, it will—and usually at the most inconvenient time, like during a presentation or when you're sipping that first coffee of the morning.

## Murphy's Law as it Applies to IT

Consider the admin who was so confident in his new backup system, he deleted the old backups—only to find the new system was more of a "back-down" system. Or the time when a server was labeled "fail-proof" by the manufacturer but decided to take an untimely vacation during peak business hours.

Why is it that printers smell fear? They wait, silent in the corner, biding their time until that critical, must-have document is needed. And then, with a mischievous whir, they flash the dreaded "out of toner" message, despite a full cartridge.

## Key Concepts: Backup

In the realm of IT, backups are your digital insurance policy. It's that parachute you hope to never use but are eternally grateful for when the time comes. How many backups does it take to keep your data safe? One more than you have.

Backups are like dental checkups—nobody enjoys them, but skipping them can lead to some serious pain down the line. And remember, a backup isn't a backup unless it's stored in at least three places: the original location, the backup location, and the "oh no, everything else failed" location.

## Disaster Recovery

Disaster recovery plans are like fire drills; they're tedious to practice but can save your bacon when things get too hot to handle. It's like rehearsing for a play where the lead actor is an unpredictable, data-eating gremlin.

And why do we encrypt our disaster recovery plans? Because the only thing worse than a system failure is a system failure with an audience. It's like having your pants fall down in public, but with more data loss.

**Incident Response**

Incident response is the IT equivalent of an emergency room, where the triage nurse is a technician deciphering critical issues from the myriad of "urgent" emails. It's about keeping your cool when the digital equivalent of "there's smoke coming from the server room" hits your inbox.

Why do incident responders always carry a USB stick? Because you never know when you'll need to jump-start a computer's heart or simply transport files in a pinch.

In the comedic theater of IT, laws aren't just rules; they're the plot twists that keep our days interesting. They remind us that while technology can be unpredictable, our preparation and responses don't have to be. So let's laugh at the chaos, secure in our knowledge of backups, and ready to tackle disasters with a smile—because in IT, the next big joke is just a power outage away.

# Chapter 14: Pop Quiz Punchlines

Grab your #2 pencils and a sense of humor—it's time to test your tech knowledge with a twist. These aren't your average practice questions; they're designed to make you think, chuckle, and most importantly, remember.

**A+ Practice Questions with a Comic Twist**

1. **Why did the computer show up at work late?**

   - A) It had a hard drive.

   - B) It lost its drive.

   - C) It had too many windows open.

   - D) It couldn't find its "keys".

   - *Tip: Remember, the boot process can be delayed by hardware issues (hard drive), software problems (too many startup programs—windows), or input errors (keyboard issues).*

2. **What do you call an antivirus that's gone rogue?**

   - A) A virus.

   - B) A feature.

   - C) Malware in disguise.

   - D) An anti-antivirus.

   - *Tip: Antivirus software acting like a virus is an example of rogue security software, a type of malicious software (malware) that deceives or misleads users.*

3. **If a network cable and a power cable were in a race, which would cause a trip first?**

- o A) The network cable, because it's always data streaming.

- o B) The power cable, because it's more grounded.

- o C) Neither, wireless technology has taken over.

- o D) Both, because proper cable management is a myth.

- o *Tip: Cable management is essential in preventing physical network issues and power faults.*

4. **Why did the RAM chip break up with the motherboard?**

- o A) It needed more space.

- o B) It couldn't handle the cycles.

- o C) It found a better slot.

- o D) The relationship was too volatile.

- o *Tip: RAM is volatile memory, meaning it requires power to maintain the stored information.*

5. **What did the tech say during an earthquake?**

- o A) "I didn't feel a thing."

- o B) "Is that the bass or just my hard drive vibrating?"

- o C) "Looks like we're having a bit of a shakeup in the server room!"

- o D) "Quick, save your work, the UPS is only going to last so long!"

    o   *Tip: An Uninterruptible Power Supply (UPS) can keep your system running briefly during a power outage, which is vital during unexpected events.*

## Tips for Remembering Key Information

- **Create Acronyms:** Just like ROY G. BIV for colors, make acronyms for tech processes or components.

- **Rhymes and Alliteration:** They're not just for poets. "If it's clicking and ticking, the hard drive needs fixing" can stick in your mind.

- **Visual Imagery:** Picture a CPU as a tiny office worker, bustling around your computer's insides, managing tasks.

- **Association:** Link new information to something you already know. Imagine a motherboard as a city map, routing data like traffic.

- **Repetition with a Beat:** Turn those tech facts into a catchy jingle, and you'll remember them like your favorite song's chorus.

By infusing humor into your study sessions with these punny questions and mnemonic devices, you'll find the information not only sticks, but it also makes the learning process a lot more enjoyable. Now, go ahead and ace that test with a smile!

# Afterword: Parting Puns and Wisdom

As we close the back cover on this compendium of chuckles and chipsets, it's important to remember that humor isn't just a way to make the bytes and bauds more bearable; it's a tool that can illuminate the motherboard path of your IT career.

**How Humor Can Continue to Aid Your IT Career**

They say laughter is the best medicine, and in the world of IT, this couldn't be truer. The ability to laugh in the face of a networking nightmare or a software snafu doesn't just ease stress; it opens up a hard drive highway of creativity, allowing you to troubleshoot with a clear mind and a light heart. A chuckle can diffuse tension, transform tech talk into layman's language, and turn a room of blank stares into a productive brainstorming session.

Embrace the lighthearted side of tech support; let your laughter reboot the dreariest days. Remember, a happy tech is a helpful tech, and a helpful tech is the one who gets the call back, the thank you card, or even just the satisfaction of a job well done—and well enjoyed.

**Encouragement for the Certification Exam**

Now, as you stand on the precipice of the A+ Certification Exam, armed with knowledge and fortified by puns, remember that this test is just another step in the grand scheme of your IT journey. It's a checkpoint, not a roadblock.

As you fill in the bubbles and click through the questions, imagine each one as a mini troubleshooting task. You've done the work, you've learned the content, and you've certainly laughed at the absurdity of it all. That humor has built neural networks in your brain, making the facts stick like Velcro.

So go forth with confidence. Step into that exam room with the same bravado as a sysadmin facing down a server room disaster. You've got this. And just think, once you're certified, you'll be the one inventing the new punchlines for the next generation of IT aficionados.

In the end, remember that IT isn't just about understanding technology; it's about understanding the people who use it. And what better way to connect with people than through a shared giggle over a geeky jest?

So, as you march forward in your IT career, keep your toolkit close and your collection of jokes closer, because sometimes, the difference between a problem and a solution is just a good laugh.

# Appendix: Jokes To Help You Pass the A+ Exam

1.  Why did the computer take a nap? Because it had too many "sleep" cycles.

2.  What's a computer's favorite snack? Microchips, of course!

3.  Why was the smartphone acting shady? It was on airplane mode and just couldn't connect with anyone.

4.  What's a computer's favorite dance move? The disk drive.

5.  Why was the computer cold? It left its Windows open!

6.  Why did the PC get glasses? To improve its web-sight.

7.  How does a computer get drunk? It takes too many screenshots.

8.  Why do motherboards have friends? Because they have good connections.

9.  Why did the computer break up with the internet? There was no "connection."

10. What do you get when you cross a computer and a lifeguard? A screensaver!

11. What do you call a group of musical hard drives? A disk-chord.

12. Why don't computers make good detectives? They can't stand a "hard drive" without crashing.

13. What's a computer's least favorite food? Spam.

14. Why did the document stay in the printer? It was jamming.

15. Why was the belt arrested? For holding up a pair of pants!

16. What's a computer's favorite ice cream? Cookies and cache.

17. Why was the computer so good at golf? Because it had a hard drive.

18. How do you know if a computer is a good singer? Check its "hardware" performance.

19. Why do programmers prefer iOS? Because they can't handle windows!

20. What's a computer's favorite state? Solid-state.

21. Why did the computer get a parking ticket? It was idling for too long.

22. Why was the computer cold? It left its Windows open.

23. Why did the computer squeak? Because someone stepped on its mouse.

24. What's a computer's favorite type of music? Heavy metal.

25. Why did the computer keep sneezing? It had a virus.

26. Why do computers make bad boxers? They always throw in the towel after a few bytes.

27. How do you comfort a JavaScript bug? You console it.

28. What did the fish say when it hit the wall? Dam.

29. Why don't some couples go to the gym? Because some relationships don't work out.

30. Why do programmers prefer dark mode? Because light attracts bugs.

31. Why did the computer go to the doctor? Because it had a Bluetooth infection.

32. Why was the JavaScript developer sad? Because he didn't Java enough coffee to stay awake.

33. What's a computer's favorite workout? Circuit training.

34. Why did the new RAM stick brag to the old hard drive? Because it was DDR4 and the hard drive was just a spinning platter.

35. What do you call a disk drive that moonlights as a DJ? The spinning platter.

36. Why was the CPU athlete upset? Because it didn't get enough cache.

37. What's a processor's life motto? "Keep calm and carry on processing."

38. Why was the motherboard worried? Because the memory sticks were going DIMM.

39. Why did the computer break up with the network? It felt too disconnected.

40. What do you call an IT teacher who touches up photos? A PDF file - "Photoshop Document Fixer."

41. Why are PCs like air conditioners? They both become useless when you open Windows.

42. Why did the computer take up gardening? To reboot its system.

43. What's a computer's favorite TV show? "Game of Thrones" – it's all about the power and the memory wars.

44. Why do power supplies never get lost? Because they always follow the current.

45. What's a computer's favorite animal? The mouse.

46. Why don't programmers like nature? It has too many bugs.

47. How do computers eat? They take bytes.

48. Why was the computer cold? It left its Windows open in safe mode.

49. Why did the computer get glasses? To improve its web-sight.

50. Why was the computer so good at golf? Because it had a hard drive.

51. Why did the computer keep sneezing? It had a virus.

52. Why was the belt arrested? For holding up a pair of pants!

53. Why did the computer get a parking ticket? It was idling for too long.

54. Why did the computer squeak? Because someone stepped on its mouse.

55. What do you call a computer floating in the ocean? A Dell Rolling in the Deep.

56. Why did the computer apply for a job? It wanted a byte at the apple.

57. What's a computer's favorite snack? Microchips and salsa.

58. Why was the smartphone wearing glasses? It lost its contacts.

59. Why was the database administrator so calm during the outage? He had his backups.

60. How do you know when a computer is getting old? When it can't keep up with the windows anymore.

And remember, while these jokes add a bit of levity to the studying process, the concepts they touch upon are crucial stepping stones on your path to becoming A+ certified. Keep smiling and keep studying!

# Appendix: A Poem to Memorize With All the Key Points to Remember to Pass the A+ Certification Exam

In the vast and virtuous land of silicon dreams, Where bytes and bits dance in luminous streams, Let us embark upon a scholarly quest, To conquer the A+ with zest and with jest.

**Stanzas of Start-Up and System Lore:**

Lo! The motherboard, in circuits arrayed, A queen in her realm, by BIOS obeyed. The POST be her herald, the beep codes her knights, Guarding the boot sequence, braving digital fights.

The CPU, a monarch, reigns supreme in his might, With cores and threads ready to take to the flight. His cache is his scepter, his clock speed, a steed, Racing through programs with unmatchable speed.

Behold RAM, the scribe, with memories fleet, In DIMMs and in modules, his tales are replete. Volatile his temper, yet swift is his pen, Recording, erasing, again and again.

**Verses on Storage and Power Divine:**

Hard drives and SSDs in chambers reside, To keep data secure, where secrets can hide. Their platters and cells in harmonious spin, Archive the world, both without and within.

The PSU, a dragon hoarding its gold, Converts mighty currents in its power hold. With volts and with watts, it feeds the great beast, Ensuring the system's electrical feast.

**Ballads of Build and Break, Configure and Cure:**

Peripherals, jesters in courtly delight, Bring joy to the realm from morning to night. Printers, scanners, and screens of all kinds, Serve at the pleasure of technical minds.

But hark! What shadow creeps yon hallowed halls? A virus, a malware, over ramparts it crawls. Fear not, brave knight, with your firewall shield, Banish the fiend, make it yield or be killed!

In networking's maze, where packets do fly, The router's decree cannot be denied. Wi-Fi doth whisper through invisible air, Binding devices with nary a care.

**A Soliloquy on Safety and Servitude Fair:**

A+ certifiers, your wisdom now gleaned, From customer service to cables well-cleaned. Document well thy deeds and thy actions, Safety and knowledge are thy main attractions.

Incident response, be thy steady hand ready, When systems do falter and screens become unsteady. Recover, restore, with backup's keen grace, And return to the realm a stable base.

So study ye well, O ye IT kin, For knowledge is power, a virtue, not sin. And with each verse remembered, each jest understood, Thou shalt pass the A+ as all good techs should.

Now, fare thee well on this noble pursuit, With a motherboard's courage and a troubleshooter's repute. May your paths be unbugged, your cycles be quick, And may your certification be ever epic!

# Glossary: Techie Talk and Terminology

Here's a byte-sized glossary for all the tech terms peppered throughout this tome, each served with a side of humor for easy digestion.

- **BIOS (Basic Input/Output System):** The BIOS is the computer's early bird, catching the POST worm before the operating system wakes up. It's the behind-the-scenes director making sure all the actors are ready before the curtain rises.

- **Boot Sequence:** This is the process your computer follows to get its act together before the big show—also known as "starting up." It's like a rocket countdown, but usually with fewer explosions.

- **CPU (Central Processing Unit):** The brain of the computer where the thinking cap sits. It processes everything from your mundane mouse clicks to the complex contemplation of cosmic calculations.

- **DIMM (Dual Inline Memory Module):** A stick of RAM, because apparently, computers get hungry for memory snacks.

- **Driver:** This isn't your Uber driver; it's the software chauffeur that helps your hardware get to its destination within the operating system.

- **Ethernet:** The autobahn of networking, where data travels on a cable freeway without the hassle of traffic lights, known as "wireless interference."

- **Firewall:** Not just a part of a car, but a digital bouncer keeping the bad Internet riff-raff out of your digital party.

- **Hard Drive:** A storage unit where your digital life is chronicled. It's like a diary that never forgets—unless it crashes.

- **HTTP (Hypertext Transfer Protocol):** The chatty Cathy of protocols that loves to talk web pages all day long.

- **Malware:** Software's evil twin that wreaks havoc, like a gremlin in the gears of your digital tranquility.

- **Motherboard:** The main stage of your computer's hardware, where the electronic ensemble comes together to perform the symphony of computing.

- **OS (Operating System):** The maestro of the computer, conducting the operations of applications and programs with the finesse of a seasoned symphony director.

- **POST (Power-On Self-Test):** The system's equivalent of a morning stretch, making sure everything is in working order before starting the day.

- **RAM (Random Access Memory):** The computer's short-term memory, where tasks are juggled like a circus act, only without the clown car.

- **Router:** The digital traffic cop, directing network packets where to go—no donuts required.

- **SSD (Solid State Drive):** A storage device that's all the rage, with no spinning disks, just speedy chips.

- **TCP/IP (Transmission Control Protocol/Internet Protocol):** The dynamic duo of Internet communication, making sure data doesn't just wander off into the digital abyss.

- **UPS (Uninterruptible Power Supply):** The superhero of power sources, saving your work from the dastardly deeds of blackouts.

- **Virus:** A digital disease looking to hitch a ride on your files and spread misery across your system—no chicken soup remedy for this.

- **Wi-Fi:** The magic that lets you browse cat videos from your couch, free from the tyranny of cables.

- **Windows:** Not just something you clean or look through, but the ubiquitous operating system that loves updates more than a news channel.

With this glossary in your pocket, you'll be fluent in tech talk, ready to crack jokes and troubleshoot with the best of them. Remember, understanding is just a term away!

# Appendix: Love at First Byte - A Ridiculously Romantic A+ Certification Saga

Once upon a silicon chip, in the motherboard of all creation, two lost souls found connection in the least likely of places—the A+ certification exam room. Here begins our tale of tech and tenderness, a story to reboot your heart and refresh your soul.

**Chapter 1: The Meet-Cute**

In a room filled with the hum of anxious students and the scent of freshly printed test papers, Sarah, a fierce warrior of the IT realm, found herself locking eyes with Jack, a bashful but brilliant tech enthusiast. Their gaze met across a row of monitors, each displaying the dreaded "Please wait for the exam to begin" message—a digital chaperone to their unexpected encounter.

**Chapter 2: The Troubleshooting Tango**

As fate would have it, Jack's computer crashed mid-exam—a blue screen of death proclaiming its digital demise. Sarah, with a heart as wide as her knowledge of system recovery, leapt from her seat to aid her distressed comrade. Together, they performed the troubleshooting tango, their hands flying over the keyboard in harmonious precision, rebooting not only the PC but also Jack's fluttering heart.

**Chapter 3: The Compatibility Query**

In the midst of defragmented hard drives and tangled network cables, a spark ignited. They found common ground in their shared disdain for obsolete software and their love for open-source romance. Jack, smitten by Sarah's ability to recite motherboard specifications, offered her a coffee, charged with the promise of endless tech support and maybe, just maybe, love.

**Chapter 4: The Firewall of Feelings**

But all was not plain sailing on the sea of love. Sarah, guarded like a well-configured firewall, was hesitant to let Jack through her port. Yet, Jack, ever the persistent troubleshooter, was determined to find the password to her heart.

## Chapter 5: The Data Backup Dance

As they danced around their feelings, backing up their emotions with layers of caution, an unexpected power outage left them in the dark. In the soft glow of emergency lights, their true feelings surged forth like an unchecked current, no UPS necessary.

## Chapter 6: The Network of Two Hearts

Hand in hand, they configured their own private network—a connection unimpeded by latency or bandwidth limitations. Their hearts, in sync, were like two hard drives in RAID 1, mirroring each other's deepest desires.

## Chapter 7: The Overclocked Emotions

Their love, much like an overclocked processor, ran hot and fast. They cooled it with laughter, jokes, and whispered sweet nothings about future tech trends, their passion encrypted in a codec only they could understand.

## Chapter 8: The Eternal Loop

In the algorithm of life, they had found their constant, their repeating loop of happiness. As they walked out of the exam room, hand in hand, certifications in the other, they knew they had passed a far greater test.

## Chapter 9: The Happily Ever After

And so, our lovebirds, bonded over a broken computer and a shared exam, embarked on a life filled with love, laughter, and lengthy Linux discussions. They proved that even in the cold, hard world of technology, the warmth of love could find a way.

## Epilogue: The System Update

Sarah and Jack, now a dynamic duo in work and in love, continue to navigate the binary seas. Their love story, like a well-written program, runs smoothly in the background of their lives, a quiet constant amidst the chaos of cables.

And thus concludes our A+ certification romance—a tale of love that started with a byte and will last a lifetime.

# Appendix: Limericks for the Learned - A+ Amusement for the Advanced

Let us dive into the depths of tech's tome, Where advanced terms and concepts freely roam. In limericks bright and ever so slick, We'll cover the A+ topics quite quick.

**On the Topic of Complex RAID Configurations:**

There once was a RAID array so vast, With disk redundancy built to last. Striped, mirrored, with parity spread, Ensuring no data was ever dead.

**Regarding the Intricacies of Virtualization:**

A VM escaped from its host one fine day, To the cloud it decided to slyly make way. It ran on resources quite thin and light, Now lives in the cloud, out of physical sight.

**The Nuances of Multimeter Use:**

With probes and a dial, the tech took a stance, To measure resistance, current, and voltage in glance. The multimeter beeped in a tone so mellow, Found a short circuit; oh, what a fine fellow!

**The Mysteries of SO-DIMM vs. DIMM:**

A SO-DIMM for laptops, so sleek and so small, While DIMMs in the desktops stood stately and tall. The memory they carry, in gigabytes dressed, Make systems run smoothly and ace every test.

**The Puzzle of Proprietary Systems and Interfaces:**

There once was a system, unique as could be, With ports and connections no one else could see. Proprietary, they said, with a smirk and a wink, Made techs everywhere scratch their heads and think.

**The Conundrum of Chipset Heat Dissipation:**

A chipset got hot, hotter than Hades, Needed a heatsink to cool off, no maybes. It dissipated heat with such grace and such flair, Kept the system cool with some thermal paste there.

**The Enigma of ECC versus Non-ECC Memory:**

ECC memory, with errors it fought, Correcting the data as it ought. But Non-ECC said with a grin, "I'm faster and cheaper, though I let errors in."

**The Chronicles of Capacitors on a Motherboard:**

On a motherboard, capacitors stand tall, Storing power, they never let it fall. But when they do burst, they give quite a show, With a pop and a fizz, off to capacitor heaven they go.

These limericks, though silly, hold knowledge quite rare, For A+ exams, they're quite the affair. So study them well, and you'll surely pass, With a chuckle, a smile, and all of your class.

# Appendix: Haikus of High Tech - The A+ Apex

In the realm of the mind, Advanced A+ concepts unwind. Haikus to enlighten.

**On the Zen of Secure Boot:**

Secure Boot guards deep, Firmware's gatekeeper, awake, No malice shall creep.

**The Esoteric UEFI:**

UEFI, Beyond BIOS's eye, Boots swift as the sky.

**The Mantra of Thermal Paste Application:**

Thin paste layer's grace, CPU's cool embrace, Heat's swift erase.

**The Mystery of x86 and ARM Architectures:**

Old x86, Meets ARM's nimble hex, Paths diverge and flex.

**The Parable of Network Topologies:**

Mesh, star, or ring dance, Data flows, a swift prance, Networks' silent chant.

**The Riddle of Cryptographic Algorithms:**

Cryptic cipher locks, Secrets safe in paradox, Keys kept in a box.

**The Labyrinth of Subnetting:**

Subnets weave their web, IPs quietly ebb, Divide and conquer.

**The Enigma of Dual-Channel Memory Configurations:**

Channels paired in time, Memory sings in rhyme, Dual paths align.

**The Serenity of ESD Precautions:**

Static whispers low, Grounding straps tied just so, Safe electrons flow.

Each haiku, a seed, Of knowledge for those who heed, Pass A+, succeed.

In circuits and code, Advanced tech concepts bestowed. Haikus guide the road.

**The Dance of Differential Backup:**

Save the changed alone, Differential's tone, Data's cornerstone.

**The Oracle of Optical Drive Types:**

Laser reads the disc, Data in a whirlwind brisk, Old tech's hieroglyph.

**The Secret of Solid-State Drives:**

No moving parts here, Silent storage frontier, Speed's pioneer.

**The Quest for Quad-Core Efficiency:**

Four cores in unison, Splitting tasks like seasoned, Powerful legion.

**The Vision of Virtual Networks:**

Networks in the cloud, Virtual, yet proud, No cables allowed.

**The Harmony of Hardware RAID Levels:**

RAID arrays entwined, Redundancy designed, Data's safety signed.

**The Wisdom of Wireless Standards:**

Signals ride the air, New standards fair, Speeds beyond compare.

**The Chant of Chipset Functions:**

Chipset's silent hum, Data's traffic drum, Through veins, it does come.

**The Whisper of Water Cooling Systems:**

Water cools the fire, Heat's silent quire, Temps never dire.

**Each haiku, a pearl, In the A+ world, Wisdom unfurled.**

Deep within the tech, Complex truths that interconnect. More haikus on deck.

**The Spirit of System Configuration:**

Settings tweaked just right, Harmony in bytes' flight, System's pure delight.

**The Enigma of ECC Memory:**

ECC stands guard, Errors barred, data starred, Reliability hard.

**The Echo of Expansion Slots:**

Slots await new cards, Expand the system's regards, Capabilities broad.

**The Quest of Quantum Computing:**

Qubits in a dance, Quantum leaps advance, Future's expanse.

**The Rhythm of RAID Reconstruction:**

When drives fail, rebuild, Data's weave, not to be killed, RAID's promise fulfilled.

**The Saga of Server Virtualization:**

Servers split in minds, Virtual space binds, Efficiency finds.

**The Whisper of Wi-Fi Encryption:**

Secret keys to trade, Wi-Fi's trust not to fade, Privacy made.

**The Dream of Dual Boot Systems:**

Two souls in one shell, OS stories they tell, Together dwell.

**The Chronicle of Cloud-Based Applications:**

Apps in the sky run, Cloud's reach has begun, Web's work is done.

Advanced concepts hold, In haikus, IT's gold, Knowledge bold, untold.

# Appendix: The A+ Bestiary - Mythical Creatures of IT Lore

In the digital forests and the silicon streams, mythical creatures roam. They are the embodiment of A+ certification concepts, each a guardian of knowledge and a beacon of wisdom.

**The Binary Basilisk:** A serpent with eyes of LED blue, Its gaze paralyzes errors in view. With a flick of its tail, the system restarts, Guarding the realms of computing arts.

*Symbol of: The critical importance of error-checking and system recovery.*

**The RAMicorn:** A beast with a mane of shimmering gold, It prances through tasks both brave and bold. With speed so swift it can outrun the night, Ensuring your memory's working just right.

*Symbol of: The significance of speedy and reliable Random Access Memory.*

**The Firewall Phoenix:** From the ashes of data breaches it rises, Wings spread wide, it strategizes. A creature that rebirths from attack and flame, Keeping intruders out of your domain.

*Symbol of: Robust network security and the resilience of a well-configured firewall.*

**The CompTIA Griffin:** Half-lion, half-eagle, in cyberspace it soars, Overseeing compliance, audits, and more. Its claws protect, its beak decrees laws, A guardian of standards without pause.

*Symbol of: The importance of adhering to industry standards and regulatory compliance.*

**The Cache Chimaera:** With heads for storage, processing, and control, It guards the cache with heart and soul. A creature of speed in the silicon rush, Keeping your access times short with a hush.

*Symbol of: The vital role of cache in system performance and speed.*

**The Defrag Dragon:** In the fragmented caverns, it breathes its fire, Aligning data with fierce desire. It roars and it rumbles, and with each blast, Your disk space is optimized at last.

*Symbol of: The necessity of regular disk defragmentation for optimal storage efficiency.*

**The Protocol Pixies:** Tiny winged folk with packets in hand, Following rules they strictly command. They dart through networks with precision and sync, Ensuring communication in a blink.

*Symbol of: The various communication protocols that keep networks running smoothly.*

**The Sovereign SSD:** A noble steed, silent and quick, It gallops through data, double-click. With no moving parts, it reigns supreme, In the land of storage, it's the king, not the queen.

*Symbol of: The advent of solid-state drives and their impact on storage technology.*

**The Thunderbolt Troll:** Under the bridge of peripheral connection, It grants speedy data transfer and protection. A troll not of trouble, but of power and might, Linking devices with thunderous delight.

*Symbol of: The power and speed of Thunderbolt technology for device connections.*

**The Virtualization Valkyrie:** Soaring through clouds, it carries the slain, From physical realms to virtual domain. It sings of efficiency, of servers reborn, In the skies of the cloud, they're no longer forlorn.

*Symbol of: The transformative power of virtualization in modern computing.*

This bestiary, though whimsical, holds true, In the world of IT, these creatures guide you. Study their habits, learn their tales, And the A+ certification you shall surely nail.

# Appendix: Proverbs and Prognostications - A Whimsical Oracle of IT Wisdom

In this digital dominion, where bytes may feast and cables coil, let us glean the wisdom of the ancients and the foretelling of the future through proverbs and prognostications that distill the essence of the IT realm.

**Proverbs of Perpetual Wisdom:**

1. "A backup a day keeps the data recovery team away." - *On the necessity of regular backups.*

2. "He who laughs last probably has a latency issue." - *Highlighting the importance of network performance.*

3. "A clean desktop is a sign of a cluttered file directory." - *Reminding us of the importance of deep organizational skills, not just surface cleanliness.*

4. "Give a man a fish, you feed him for a day; teach a man to use Google, and he may never bother you again." - *Stressing the importance of self-help skills in IT.*

5. "A watched pot never boils, and a watched loading screen never loads." - *On the perception of time in relation to computer processes.*

6. "The early bird gets the worm, and the early coder catches the bug." - *Encouraging thorough and timely debugging.*

7. "One man's trash is another man's treasure; one user's deleted files are another's data recovery exercise." - *The value of understanding data restoration.*

8. "Too many cooks spoil the broth; too many apps slow the boot." - *Highlighting the need for efficient startup processes.*

9. "A stitch in time saves nine; a well-placed comment saves debug time." - *On the importance of commenting code.*

**Prognostications of Fabled Foresight:**

1. "In the land where the cloud reigns supreme, the sky is not the limit, but the beginning." - *Predicting the continued growth of cloud computing.*

2. "The time shall come when the paper shall fear, for the printer shall become as rare as the tech-savvy seer." - *Foreseeing the move towards paperless environments.*

3. "A great shift approaches, where not the loudest but the most encrypted voice shall be heard." - *Emphasizing the future importance of encryption.*

4. "Behold the era when machines learn to learn; the troubleshooter's role, ever more discern." - *On the rise of machine learning and AI in IT.*

5. "Look to the day when no cable shall tether, and all devices shall communicate as birds of a feather." - *Envisioning a future dominated by wireless technology.*

6. "The time is nigh when security shall not be a moat, but a spell cast around data, both seen and remote." - *Predicting advancements in cybersecurity measures.*

7. "The day will dawn where virtual reality blends with our own, and help desks shall troubleshoot a whole new unknown." - *Anticipating challenges in emerging VR technologies.*

Let these ancient bytes of wisdom and forward-looking visions guide you through the circuits of your IT endeavors, for in the world of technology, to be forewarned is to be forearmed. With these proverbs and predictions, may your path to A+ certification—and beyond—be as clear as a well-documented script.

# Appendix: A Solemn Prayer to the Lords of IT for A+ Enlightenment

In the hallowed glow of monitor light, we bow our heads and beseech the Lords of IT, those paragons of packets and paladins of processors, to bestow upon us the wisdom of the motherboard and the courage of the cursor as we embark upon the sacred rite of A+ certification.

**Invocation:**

Oh mighty Lords of IT, who art in the server clouds, Hallowed be thy frameworks, thy circuits, and thy shrouds. We, your humble students, seekers of the byte, Invoke your presence, your power, and your light.

**Petition for Knowledge:**

Grant us clarity of mind, like a freshly defragged drive, And focus sharp as a laser printer, that we may thrive. Bestow upon us the memory of a top-tier RAM, To recall all we have studied, the answers to exam.

**Request for Understanding:**

Bestow upon us the understanding, deep and clear, Of motherboards and modems, which we hold so dear. May we navigate file systems, vast and wide, And conquer every question that the test may provide.

**Appeal for Serenity:**

In the face of perplexing prompts and confounding queries, Grant us the serenity of a well-cooled chassis. Should we encounter the dreaded blue screen of despair, Remind us of the CTRL+ALT+DEL prayer.

**Benediction for Success:**

And when the hour comes to prove our worth, To demonstrate the knowledge we've gathered on Earth, Bless our pencils and scansheets with your guiding grace, That we may fill in bubbles with accuracy and pace.

**Closing Doxology:**

We ask for your blessings, O mighty IT host, To pass our A+ with scores to boast. With your guidance, we shall not fear nor falter, As we approach the sacred altar.

So let it be typed, so let it be done, From the first boot-up to the setting sun. In the name of the Router, the Switch, and the Holy LAN, Amen.

May this prayer echo in the data centers of eternity, and may its echoes guide us through the labyrinth of diagnostics and beyond the veil of user errors. Let the Lords of IT watch over all who endeavor to master their craft and ascend the ranks of certified professionals. Amen.